The Bookkeeper Superhero

Natasha Everard

DEDICATION

For my parents, husband Mat, and son Leo.

CONTENTS

ACKNOWLEDGEMENTS

To my parents, husband Mat, and son Leo: Thank you for the steadfast support you've provided throughout this incredible journey. Your belief in me has been my awesome, and I couldn't have done it without you.

To Emily Wells, Nicola Mason, and Yulia Taylor: Your unwavering support and boundless encouragement have been the wind beneath my wings. I'm immensely grateful for your friendship and guidance.

To Lara Manton, Amanda Lang & Samantha Mitcham: You've been inspirational superheroes in my life. Your strength and determination have shown me the way, and I'm forever thankful for your influence.

Finally, to AutoEntry by Sage: Thank you for believing in me and helping turn my dream into reality. Your support has been instrumental in making this book come to life.

With deep appreciation,

Natasha

Winner of **Institute of Certified Bookkeepers LUCA Awards**

Expenses and Document Management Software of the Year
2018 & 2019

&

Data and Expenses App of the Year
2021, 2022 & 2023

FOREWORD BY
CHRIS DOWNING

Part of my job involves travelling the UK and supporting events for accounting professionals.

It's when attending bookkeeping events that I often have the most fun.

Why? Bookkeepers exist on the more personal side of accounting. They work very closely with their clients and form strong relationships that turn into friendships more often than not.

Yet as Natasha explains in this book, often bookkeepers are the ultimate sole practitioners, existing as a team of just one, and typically in home offices.

It's perhaps because of this that they tend to be very sociable when gathered together, and also tend to be generous with their time and resources, especially when amongst their own kind. I've glad to have benefitted from this at events and also in my earlier professional life when I worked as an accountant.

Nowadays, as Product Director for accounting services and tools at the software company Sage, there's another reason I admire bookkeepers. It's because of the way they continually embrace technology to empower what they do.

Again, this comes down to the sole practitioner nature of their businesses. Data entry automation via tools like AutoEntry by Sage is a basic requirement rather than an optional extra, for example. Who has time to manually key in the data from hundreds of client bank statements, invoices and receipts?

And so, I was honoured when Natasha asked me to write the foreword for her new book that explains how to become the ultimate bookkeeping superhero.

She would hate to hear me say it, but Natasha cuts an impressive figure in the bookkeeping community.

The growth of her own practice has coincided with the growth of the Facebook community she created to offer support to those who, like her, exist as a formidable team of one. With over 12,000 members, and getting larger every day, this community has proved welcoming and invaluable to accounting professionals.

As she says, there's no such thing as a stupid question, and there's always time to share some sunshine with others.

Bookkeeping is a rewarding career but, more than this, for many people it's also an ideal vocation that lets them work to the beat of their own drum, and in a way that fits with their lifestyle. I'm excited that Natasha's put her wisdom and experience into words in this book so that more will be empowered to join the growing revolution this sector represents.

Chris Downing
Product Director, Sage
and **Institute of Certified Bookkeepers Honorary Companion**

HOW TO READ
THIS BOOK

This book is written as if taking place across a working week—from Monday, all the way through to Friday.

It's not *really* a guide to an actual working week, of course. Instead, I've simply used the metaphor of a working week as a concise way of explaining the core principles behind bookkeeping as I know them (and also to share my experiences).

The chapters are as follows:

1. **Motivational Monday**: Before you start you need to figure out your setup. This includes figuring our why you want to become an accounting professional, but it also includes getting your workspace right. That's what this chapter is all about.

2. **Timing Tuesday**: A core skill for bookkeeping is managing your time, as well as that of others. Get it right and everything else will fall into place. This chapter explains everything I've learned about time management for bookkeepers.

3. **Workload Wednesday**: Digging down into a typical working day is the purpose of this chapter, and I share my hard-won methods for ensuring you maximise what you can get out of every hour.

4. **Throwback Thursday**: Being able to review what you're doing, to make improvements for yourself and others (as well as avoiding all the pitfalls), is an often-overlooked skill. And this chapter goes into depth.

5. **Feelgood Friday**: This chapter is about more than just getting ready for the coming week. It's about getting support, and finding your tribe. It's also about the skill required to make time to realise what a great job you're doing!

6. **Weekend reflections**: This is a short conclusion of the book with some notes about where you can find me and my projects online.

So, what are you waiting for? Jump straight in with the first day of the week and ensure that your first Monday delivers the motivation you need…

MOTIVATIONAL MONDAY

This is the first chapter, and as such, it's probably of most interest to those who are starting out in our profession, or perhaps are fairly new to our industry and need to build some confidence.

Alternatively, it might be useful for those who've been longer in the role but have been winging it until now!

I'm going to discuss what you need to be able to set up shop and operate as a bookkeeper.

This could be what we might call hard infrastructure, such as the tech. It might getting the right qualifications, and ensuring you keep on top of your development.

But before all that, it's about understanding who you are, and why you're doing this.

Who are you?

The first question is one that can be surprising hard to answer.

You might want to rush straight to creating a business plan. Or maybe your first thought is to rush straight to creating a page on Instagram to let the world know that you're here. Old timers might visit the Companies House website and register a limited company, I guess!

But stop for a minute.

What are you going to be? Are you going to be a bookkeeper, or are you going to work more in the accountancy area? Maybe you envision a transition between the two, or a merging of professions, much as you'll hear our colleagues at the ICB suggest nowadays. That's fine. But the key thing is that you need to work through these thoughts and plans right now, and not 12 or 24 months down the line.

Are you going to target a certain set of clients in a particular industry? Maybe you love working in e-commerce, for example. Well, it's a growing area. But if you don't decide who your clients are going to be from day one then you might be casting your net too wide, and leading yourself to work with people you're just incompatible with.

Plus, don't forget the collateral benefits of specialising, such as how word of mouth between people with similar interests can form a big part of your marketing.

Brainstorm all of this. But be targeted when you do so. When I started, I brainstormed less about *how* I was going to run the business. I wanted to answer my *why*.

- Why did I want to work as a bookkeeper?

- Why did I want to work for myself?

- What was I trying to achieve?

- Why did I choose the path of sole practitioner?

This wasn't about money, perhaps surprisingly. I wanted to avoid having a boss. I wanted more time to myself. I wanted to be able to choose who I worked with. And most importantly, I wanted to choose the times I worked. All of this told me *why*.

And without that, I wouldn't be able to move any further in my planning. Everything leads out of that simple question. I couldn't fit in any other parts that make the whole package without knowing this.

What's in a name?

Next, you have to decide what to name your business. What's in a name? Well, people tend to merge their personality with their business. And that's great! But in bookkeeping, this is perhaps even more pronounced. Your branding is your personality. It's how your clients will see you. After all, in the first instance, most of them will encounter your name first.

And in bookkeeping it's almost like you're an employee for many of the firms that work with you. They trust you like they trust an employee, and rely

> *... in bookkeeping it's almost like you're an employee for many of the firms that work with you ...*

upon you to keep their business running. You remove the stresses and strains for them. It's very personal.

I've had many clients who have become friends, and that's very much the nature of our profession.

So, what you call yourself advertises your personality, and helps people understand what you're about.

My first business name was NME Bookkeeping. That's my initials, in case you haven't guessed! But when I read it out to people, I kept saying "enemy bookkeeping"! Who wants to work with an enemy? It was certainly quirky, but not in the right way.

Now, my birthday is on Halloween. I love all things that go bump in the night—ghost stories and things like that. And that's where my business name, Bewitching Bookkeeping, came from.

Now that was a little bit of me in my business, but I was able to take it to a new level. I say that I "take the mystery out of bookkeeping". I tell people I take the bookkeeping mess and "magically" make it disappear, before making it reappear all in order!

I'm also launching a new side to my business where I help fellow sole practitioner bookkeepers and accountants, and I'm calling that project The Maverick Revolution. Again, this communicates what I'm about—helping the "Lone Rangers" of the industry. It helps me stand out. (See *Weekend Reflections* later in this book for details.)

So, in summary you're setting your own goals in the business when you choose a name that works 100% for you. It doesn't matter what others think because ultimately you need a brand that you can be passionate about. Get this right and it'll shine through in your everyday business activities.

Certifications

There are various routes when it comes to training and becoming certified.

Most people go through the Institute of Certified Bookkeepers (ICB), Association of Accounting Technicians (AAT) or Institute of Accountants and Bookkeepers (IAB). The benefits of this are that you get ongoing support, such as information about new developments.

Personally, I trained and am now anti-money laundering (AML) supervised by HMRC. I stick to the things that I'm qualified for, and have experience in—bookkeeping, tax returns, payroll, and VAT. That's it. I don't do anything else.

Ours isn't a profession like solicitors, where there's very tight regulation and requirements on who can operate. Ultimately the path you choose for certification and training is down to what's right for you, and what you want to achieve with your business.

I discuss this in more detail later in this chapter, but the key points that you must have before accepting any paid work are:

- Anti-Money Laundering (AML) supervision, either with an awarding body or directly with the HMRC.

- Indemnity insurance.

- Registration with the Information Commissioner's Office (ICO) for data protection.

And ultimately, those qualifications and/or experience in the services you are providing.

Bookkeeper qualities

If you're considering bookkeeping as a career, I'd say you need three main qualities:

1. **Resilience:** Anybody who's going to be a sole practitioner needs to be resilient. In any business you're going to have ups and downs. For example, the pandemic knocked us all for six. And there are constantly changing requirements for what bookkeepers can do for businesses. For example, Making Tax Digital is huge. But the key thing is that you need to not only accept and ride out these ups and downs, but also learn from them. That may as well be a definition of business resilience.

2. **Methodical:** This one might sound obvious, but you need to be good at record keeping. Much of your work is organising data in a way that will let you continue your business and avoid your client have the stress of having to take care of this themselves. Tech really comes to the forefront here, because often this is a matter of uploading things for your client, rather than them doing it. It's all part of the mindset of being methodical.

3. **Adaptability:** This is less about clients, and more about protecting you and your business. You setup as a sole practitioner because you want to run your business your way. But don't forget that clients you work with have probably setup their own businesses because they wanted to work *their* way. So, it becomes all about finding a match. If you want to run your business your way, then make sure you find clients that fit that way as well. Not all clients will. This is that's why there are thousands of bookkeepers all over the world. We all do a good job and that's because we are all different and suit different clients. But being able to adapt to your own way of working in that you can say, "No, thank you," to a new client who doesn't fit, is a key skill.

The bookkeeper's lifestyle

Nine times out of 10, bookkeeping is done on an historical basis. You're looking at data from things that happened days ago, or longer. You're not having to respond immediately to developments, unlike many professions.

There are certainly deadlines, but these often work very well around the lifestyles of young parents, or people who are switching roles and learning bookkeeping on a part-time basis. There are many people who come into bookkeeping this way.

Again, we're back to the simple premise that bookkeeping is one of the few professions that allows you run things your way, and grow the business on your terms. You can work one or two hours a week, and pick the right client(s) that will fill that. Or if you have 20 hours a week then you've got the option to grow even more.

Working around a small family, or if you have other kinds of care needs, or even if you just prefer to have a more satisfying work/life balance compared to many people today: bookkeeping will work with you.

My own start in bookkeeping comes from being an Accounts Manager, employed in a company. I was approached by a friend who said they knew somebody who needed bookkeeping doing, and I was asked if I would like to do it.

And so, I started part-time, just doing it on Saturday mornings. And I did this for a few years, carrying on with my main Accounts Manager job.

... getting the right clients for me was all part of the initial growth ...

The bookkeeping work consumed more of my time, and, at the same moment, I was starting to realise: I don't like working in a firm! I don't like working for somebody! It made me feel awkward. My anxiety became a problem, and the stress from my 9-5 job had begun making me feel ill.

After having just two clients for many years for whom I'd been doing part-time bookkeeping, I decided to take a leap of faith. And it snowballed from there!

Getting the right clients for me was all part of the initial growth I've mentioned earlier, when I was trying to figure out my "why". I brainstormed around thoughts such as why I liked a certain client, and why I liked another client perhaps less. This defined me as a bookkeeper and as somebody who operated a business.

The evolving role

Bookkeeping can be a creative role, and that's a useful skill to have because ours is also a profession that's been evolving and changing over recent years.

Think about Covid and the pandemic lockdowns. Believe it or not, my business grew during that period. People were desperate for help and to decipher the help the government was offering. And they valued those of us who were able to go the extra mile to ensure they didn't feel isolated or alone.

But more importantly, Covid flipped the bookkeeping and accounting industry on its head. At one time, attending client premises (being "on-prem") was a key part of the job. But because Covid taught us the value of working from home, and made people less afraid to use tech like Zoom and cloud-enabled data sharing, most bookkeepers now rarely leave our home offices. This is true of many professions, but it's certainly benefited bookkeeping more than many.

Covid turned what we might've expected to be 10 years of technological advancement into just 10 days! And this has benefitted bookkeeping so much.

It's why the bookkeeping industry has become a good choice of profession for a lot of people. We've shown ourselves to be not afraid of technology. We're not afraid of learning and earning our CPD (Continual Professional Development). We're not afraid of standing up against accountants and declaring ourselves their partners—they do one thing, we do another.

Our work with accountants is increasingly important. We're a team providing our clients with a full service, and with Making Tax Digital for income tax being introduced in a few years, this is no bad thing. We're perfectly aligned for the future.

Furthermore, because bookkeepers nowadays have fewer expectations to be on-prem for our clients, our prospective client base opens up to the entirety of the UK.

Getting the right infrastructure

The great news is that bookkeeping needs very little expenditure upfront. Many of us can and do work from a home office, and use our existing laptops and mobile phones.

But you need to consider your needs. What kind of bookkeeper are you going to be? For example, if you intend to do face-to-face meetings with clients then you'll need to be able to do that—whether that's having transport or, if the client is coming to you, a dedicated space.

In terms of workspace, you need to find what works best for you. There's no right way of doing it. There are people who find a desk in a café and work from there. You might hot desk in a shared space. However, you should take care around data protection requirements. People can peer at your screen over your shoulder. In fact, I would suggest you avoid client work if you're in any kind of shared space, and do other kinds of work instead.

For me, I realised that I would need a dedicated desk at home that was my own. It needed to be in a quiet place, away from children and pets! Crucially, I don't mention my location anywhere. So, I sometimes work from my parents' house, or cafes.

I realised during Covid that I really needed a dedicated internet connection for my home office. Everything bookkeepers do is in the cloud nowadays, so this is simply vital. My son was at home during lockdown and would often max-out the connection while playing on his Xbox, or downloading files, or streaming from school. Getting my own independent internet connection turned out to be simple: I signed-up for 4G broadband. This is like having a permanent mobile phone connection for your computers, so it doesn't need a cable to your home, or phone line. Therefore, there's very little setup, too.

Consider your schedule. Are you going to keep to a strict 9-5? Or are you simply going to start when you're feeling ready, and finish following the same rules, with the proviso being only that the work gets done?

Some people choose to have certain days where they only work solidly, and the phone is set to send calls straight through to voicemail and the email app is closed.

Consider safety, too. You might be working from home during the daytime when family members are out. You might find that clients have to drop things off for you, such as bundles of paperwork. My home/office is in the middle of nowhere, and the nearest people to me are dead people in a churchyard! However, I have a video doorbell system, so I can see who's at the door each time.

Finally, do make sure that you're legally permitted to work from home. For example, many rental properties don't let people run a business from the home, although home working is usually considered OK. It might be as simple as just running it past your landlord first. Check your home insurance policies, too. Again, working from home for an employer is usually OK but running an actual business from the address might invalidate the terms.

Hard infrastructure

Make sure you have a budget plan when you start, so that you don't start spending uncontrollably. Even small purchases here and there can add-up.

But ultimately, our industry is one that simply doesn't have a lot of capital expenditure and fixed costs. It's relatively economic when starting out.

Here's a few tips around what I personally use to run my bookkeeping business, and the costs associated with it:

- **Mobile phone**: I use my personal mobile but with an e-SIM for my business number, and a normal SIM card for my personal calls. Most modern mobile phones allow this configuration. If in doubt, speak to the phone manufacturer's support team, or your mobile provider's helpline. Another option is voice-over-IP apps that let you rent a UK number. These are just like the existing phone app on your phone, but for me, it's means just one phone I take everywhere.

- **Computer**: I started my business with my own laptop, and I kept using that for four years. During Covid I decided to get a more powerful computer, and nowadays I use multiple monitors. I find this is better for automation work, which

I'll cover in a different chapter of this book. But none of this extra hardware is strictly necessary. In fact, one thing that pushed me towards buying the extra screens was because they were on sale, and I couldn't resist the bargain!

- **Scanner**: I invested in a business scanner in order to get data from documents and into AutoEntry by Sage, my financial data automation tool of choice. The scanner was a large investment, by the standards we're discussing here, costing a little over £300. But it's been a very useful tool.

- **AML licence**: As I mentioned earlier, every year you'll need to get an anti-money laundering (AML) practice licence, either through your awarding body (e.g., the ICB), or direct from HMRC. This is around £300-£350, and usually needs to be paid as a lump sum rather than monthly.

- **Data protection fee**: Currently this is £40 a year and is paid to the ICO. It's a legal requirement for any business that processes personal information. And bookkeeping definitely falls into that category.

- **Indemnity insurance**: This is a fixed fee each month, and in recent times this has increased, just like all insurances have, such as car or home insurance. Insurance cost vary, and I suggest you speak to either a broker, or to those your governing body recommend. If you do have clients visit your home, you may need to take a look at other insurances, too, that may be applicable.

- **Software subscriptions**: As I've mentioned, most software nowadays is in the cloud, and usually it's paid for by monthly or yearly subscriptions. There's two ways to handle this. You can pay for the apps and work this cost into the prices you charge clients. Or your clients can pay for the software themselves and provide access (or the output from the apps) for you. Sometimes there are partnership programmes that provide a happy middle ground, where the bookkeeper can actually earn money or credits by offering their clients the apps to use themselves. AutoEntry offers a scheme like this, for example.

Business plan

You'll need a business plan but, perhaps surprisingly, I don't believe you need feel stressed if you either don't have one from day one, or if you have one but feel it's incomplete. You can fill in the gaps as you progress. Some of these gaps you won't even know until you start working for your first client, so this makes sense.

... your business plan is valuable because it will remind you of your "why" ...

A great tip is to use artificial intelligence (AI) tools like ChatGPT or Google Bard to create your business plan. Just ask it to create, say, a three-year business plan for a British or UK bookkeeper. It's stunning what it comes back with, and you should certainly be able to use this as a template for your business plan, at least. It might be all you need!

You'll need a method statement, which is what you can take to clients to give clarity on how you're going to work. Here's where you list the technology you're going to use, like automation, and things like that.

Your business plan is valuable because it will remind you of your "why", as we discussed right at the beginning of this chapter. It'll also break down your financial targets, so you'll know if your business is doing well.

But financial targets are also more concrete. The issue with bookkeeping is, as I said earlier, it can be an up-and-down existence. You have to be prepared to ride the crest of the wave and accept that some periods will be better than others. Some clients may stay with you for 10 or 20 years. Some might not last 20 minutes! Financial targets help you keep an eye on where you should be heading for.

Furthermore, our industry has no happy norm when it comes to income, with people charging based on what they feel works best. Location plays a big factor, too, as does whether you're a sole practitioner compared to the services of a big firm.

As a sole practitioner, there's no hard limit on the maximum number of clients you have, and that you want to aim for in your plan. It's all about the workload the clients you have present to you. For example, you might have 100 clients, but they're all Self Assessment income taxpayers. So, the work is largely a single touchpoint during the year.

Or you might have 10 clients, and each could demand nearly all of your time, every day!

Here's what I'd expect to include in any business plan for a bookkeeper:

- **Year 1**: 5-10 clients. Pricing will cover your expenses, plus the net income afterwards that you're hoping to achieve.

- **Year 2**: Up to 30 clients.

- **Year 3**: Expect to plateau at this point. Maybe you might marginally boost client numbers, but this is the point where you'll be starting to work out what clients you like to work with, plus what industries you prefer working with.

- **Years 4 and 5**: This is the point at which you can expect growth once again. You'll have figured out what's worked, and what doesn't work.

TIMING
TUESDAY

In this second chapter we look at timing and, specifically, we look at managing time across the workday.

A team of one

As a sole practitioner, one way to view it is to consider yourself a team of one. And you need to manage that team, even if it's just you.

But across the day you'll be undertaking various tasks, so you could also say you're the manager of a team—a bookkeeper, a marketing executive, a client support worker, and so forth. You're the janitor all the way up to the CEO! And each role requires a little consideration around time and resource management.

You're also working as a part of several different teams, as an extension of your clients' businesses. Even if your client is a sole trader then you'll be forming a team of two— you, and them!

This can often mean there's elements of client management and discovery, in terms of managing your client's time when it comes to accounting tasks. After all, if you don't get what you need from the client in a timely fashion then you can do very little for them. Even worse, a haphazard client, supplying data at random, can be ruinous for your schedule.

The automation software you use in your practice can effectively be a second employee working alongside you, too. I call this Software-as-an-Employee, which plays on the commonly used term Software-as-a-Service (or SaaS), and it clearly demonstrates how software for the modern bookkeeper is so very vital.

You must manage how you use the software, in terms of timing, to get the most from it and again protect your own schedule so you're maximally effective. You need to learn when's the best time to assign the software tasks.

This also allows more time for you to be the human. You're freed-up to provide the human touch, and the interaction that clients value—and that's also offers the best route forward for growing your practice.

Digital clients

Here in the UK, the big development recently affecting all bookkeepers and accountants has been Making Tax Digital. This government initiative legally mandates clients use digital record keeping for their taxes, and make tax return submissions, too.

So far, it's been rolled out for VAT, and in a few years' time it'll be rolled out for income tax and Self Assessment. Following that it'll be rolled out for Corporation Tax. That's the extent of the plans so far revealed by HMRC, but it's not hard to imagine other taxes like Inheritance Tax one day falling within its boundaries, too.

MTD for VAT was a difficult transition back when it was introduced in 2019, but it forced VAT-registered clients to go digital with their accounting much more quickly than would've happened organically.

And this is what we need as accountants. We need our clients to be unafraid of digital technologies, because that's how they're going to communicate with us, and send us the data we need.

Plus, it's how we're going to manage their time and resources when it comes to working with us.

Dare I say it, but the Covid pandemic helped too, making useful tools like the Zoom videoconferencing software a near-standard feature of phones and laptops.

So, step one in managing your client's time is to get them to go digital for their accounting. You then need to manage how the clients use those digital tools, so that they're a part of the process—and so that they *want* to be part of the process, too. Any client who has opted-in to your processes is the best kind of client!

Automation and time management

Automation is the way forward. Nowadays, terrific tools like AutoEntry not only banish many accounting work processes, but also provide a great example of how you can work with clients to

> *... AutoEntry enables the bookkeeping to become digital quickly, and it also takes a lot of mystery out of the bookkeeping process for the client ...*

manage time better. You manage how the app is used, and the rewards follow naturally.

AutoEntry means clients can snippet pictures of expenses, while on the go using their mobile phone. The accounting data is automatically extracted, and it then comes to your desktop, where you can then process it and publish it through to the client's ledgers.

I tell clients using AutoEntry is as simple as taking a selfie. For example, I've got a client who works in construction. On a visit to his wholesaler, he can either take a snapshot of the printed receipt when he gets back to his van, or he can forward the email containing the receipt to his special AutoEntry email address. Either way the data and an image of the receipt then comes to me.

It's also possible to scan-in receipts, invoices or statements on the desktop and pass them to AutoEntry for extraction, which is what I do when clients send me paperwork.

AutoEntry enables the bookkeeping to become digital quickly, and it also takes a lot of mystery out of the bookkeeping process for the client. One of the biggest boosts is that they can't lose a receipt, and that little image of the receipt stays in the software for however long it's needed—say six years for income tax.

One client I work with has hundreds of invoices from the same supplier each month. These tend to end-up here, there and everywhere, and I can never be sure I get every one of them. AutoEntry has a supplier statement reconciliation feature, and it takes seconds to reconcile the supplier account, and then tell me what's missing. Previously, that would take four or five days.

This is great for me in terms of managing my time, but for the client it also means they can stay on top of their expenditure. Everything's more accurate, there's no risk of data becoming hidden (by accident or deliberately!), and the client can forecast ahead, too.

In the next chapter I'll talk about how we can use tools like AutoEntry to ensure our daily workflow runs smoothly.

Client discovery

A part of your work initially with any client is around discovery. You need to talk to them and probe them. You need to find out what kind of deadlines they have, and when they're due. You need to ask questions about their existing bookkeeping to try and discover the pacing they prefer, and what kind of touchpoints they have with their bookkeeping and accounting, as well as how many.

Are they good with technology? How automated are they already? What potential do they have for taking this further (e.g., are they a Luddite? Or do they show signs of already embracing tech, such as making good use of their mobile for personal stuff?).

This isn't just about time management. It's also about figuring out the job costing. If a client is going to be more demanding of your time, then you need to take this into consideration. As I discuss later in this chapter, some clients might not even be viable for you.

From your own perspective, you need to figure out how this new client will fit into your personal deadlines. For example, for the VAT returns I handle each month, all of my client returns need to be completed and submitted by the 15th. So, I stagger the deadlines I provide to clients for their paperwork to ensure I have the capacity. And I then stagger when I'll process and submit each return.

I also use technology to send out automated email reminders to my clients to ensure they collate and send through the documents I require.

Educating clients about going digital

Here are some things you can tell your clients to help nudge them towards adopting technology, in order to better manage their time when working with you:

- **Sustainability**: In the old days you might drive to a client premises, and sit there for a few hours using a computer they provide, crunching through a stack of paperwork. Or the client might drive to you to drop off paperwork. Going digital removes the need for mileage, and you can use the same single computer for every client. It removes the need even for paperwork in the first place if you do it right (although even this far into the 21st century, a paperless office remains a pipe dream—you'll still need a filing cabinet or two in your workplace).

- **Legal requirements**: Like it or loathe it, HMRC wants us all to have digital accounting. MTD legally mandates this, and there's no opting out of it, outside of a handful of fringe cases based on genuine need or limitations (e.g., your client's physical or mental condition makes complying with MTD impossible, or they live in a remote location where there's no internet). In other words, digitisation is inevitable. Why wait until the last minute when the government forces you to do so?

- **Making life easier**: Digital accounting is just easier for everybody. Yes, those processes that your client uses right now—like stuffing folders full of invoices and receipts—might feel like the easiest choice. But the reality is that they're just immediate solutions. In the long term they're actually time consuming, and swapping in a digital process can save almost unbelievable amounts of time. People who use AutoEntry say it reduces the time spent on data entry processes by 90%. Days previously spent inputting data turn into just hours, or hours spent on that turn into just minutes.

- **Accuracy**: Digital technology allows us to increase accuracy without even trying. For example, mistyping numbers into accounting software—known as fat finger syndrome—is much more common than we'd all like to admit. But using an app like AutoEntry means you can get up to 99% verified accuracy. This accuracy can also mean a lower chance of penalties from HMRC should the client end-up being audited.

More challenging clients

Of course, there are clients who just will never go digital. They may own a mobile phone but use the most basic models, and never do much more than actually make calls using it. They don't have email, and they don't use the web.

A lot of bookkeeper and accountant clients are farmers from the older generation, for example. Now, there are many modern and progressive farmers making excellent use of technology. But it does seem to be an industry where you find a good number of people at the more reticent end of the spectrum.

My experience is often that clients like this won't go digital, no matter how much you nudge them, or educate them about how it's about making life easier for them, as well as you. It's simply not an option.

Sometimes a client might be reluctant because there are things they want to hide, or they're scared because their existing accounting is such a mess, and they suspect they haven't been fully compliant in the past.

Maybe these kinds of clients aren't right for you. Sometimes you just have to be brutal. You can't manage the time of a non-digital client, and in fact, attempting to do so just consumes more of your work time.

But do explore alternatives before making that decision. Even if you can just get the client to activate open banking, for example, then that could be a game changer when you're handling their accounting because you'll be able to reconcile much more easily. The client doesn't have to be technical to do this and it could involve just a single call to their bank.

You may have to think outside the box with difficult clients, and be creative. For example, in preparation for the introduction or MTD for Income Tax and Self Assessment (MTD ITSA) in a few years' time, I'm creating an additional service offering whereby clients are provided with prepaid packaging. I'm exploring options with courier firms to find a secure way of doing this, because that's obviously a key element. But the client will periodically send me their paperwork like invoices, receipts and statements. I'll then process it using AutoEntry and send it all right back to them.

This will be priced into my fees, and I use GoProposal by Sage to ensure that the initial letter of engagement explains all of this, and to consistently price my clients and future clients.

Managing your time

In addition to managing your clients' time through the applied use of clever software and apps, you also have to set boundaries. These need to be communicated to clients.

When I setup my practice, I didn't get this. I answered the phone whenever it rang, whether that was weekends, evenings, or night-time. It felt great having all the engagement with clients. It felt like work.

But it was a huge mistake in hindsight.

Distractions are the biggest theft of our time. They make time disappear. They can also lead to procrastination, which is to say, not making effective use of your time. Checking emails is relatively easy and feels like it offers

... when using software, I imagine that I have an employee to whom I assign certain tasks on certain days ...

immediate results in terms of achieving things. Our brains are naturally drawn to this, often pushing aside more difficult tasks to allow it.

A few years ago, I had an episode where I forgot I was self-employed. I let myself be dictated to by everybody else. I worked to their schedule, almost like I was literally one of their employees. I forgot why I became a sole practitioner, which is to work by my own rules.

You can't pour from an empty cup, and I found that other people kept pouring out my cup without me realising.

With all the above in mind, I've learned how to block time. There are times when I don't accept calls, and don't check emails, and just do the bookkeeping tasks that need to be done that month. I go into detail about this in the next chapter.

I put my phone into Do Not Disturb mode (I use an e-Sim for work calls on my personal phone—see the previous chapter).

There are only certain times in the day when I check my emails. For me, this is 8.30am, 1pm, and then 4.30pm, although you might find other schedules work best. I still get urgent messages, of course, but I only deal with them during those times. And in reality, I find nothing is ever so urgent that it must be dealt with the moment an email is sent and then received by me.

I'll talk more about my typical workday in the next chapter, but when using software, I imagine that I have an employee to whom I assign certain tasks on certain days, using the knowledge of my client requirements.

And just like with an employee, I expect the results to be ready when I need them. As just one example, in the first week of the month I upload client bank statements to AutoEntry. Then, the next week I have the data ready for checking for VAT return deadlines for the clients.

So, I assign tasks to software just as I assign tasks to employees. I am the CEO for the software I use! I see it this way, rather than simply "using" an app or software. And this really helps me manage my time and effectively fill out my weekly schedule.

Tasks to assign your software "employee"

Here are some of the tasks that I get software to help with each week.

Some of these involve exploring all the features in software, and I'm a huge advocate of this. If you pay for software then you owe it to yourself to get every possible feature out of that software, and it's up to you to learn how via support materials or training, or just keeping your ear close to the ground to see what others say about using the app on social media, for example.

Here's my list:

- **Keying-in data from paperwork**: As I've mentioned, tools like AutoEntry are a backbone of the work I do. I can upload receipts and invoices in the afternoon, for example, and know that the data will be extracted and waiting for me the next morning for publishing through to accounts software. And I use the statement reconciliation feature for clients each month to ensure I have everything I need.

- **Bank account reconciliation**: Nearly all accounting apps nowadays feature automated reconciliation features, of varying sophistication. Some involve AI, for example, to try and match brand new transactions that appear on the bank statement. Using automated bank reconciliation is less about handing off the task to your software employee, though, and more like standing over their shoulder to make sure they're doing it right. But it's still a big-time saver compared to manually comparing invoices, receipts and purchase orders against the bank statement.

- **Document collection**: I can get my software employee to visit clients to get their paperwork… Virtually, of course. Cloud storage services like DropBox allow you to provide clients with an email address, or a link for uploading. But with the email address, all the client needs to do is forward any bills or receipts they receive to that address (a feature also available in tools like AutoEntry, by the way, which again can save a lot of time).

- **Sending emails**: Even humble old Microsoft Outlook has automation built in nowadays. Sometimes I remember that I need to email a client about something, but it turns out to be 7am just after I've got up, or 10.30pm just as I'm preparing for bed! Well, Outlook lets me schedule the send of emails. I write the email, and then choose I want to send it at, say, 9am the next morning. The client knows no difference, and assumes I've sent it at that time. It's also a good idea to use practice management software to schedule reminder emails. For example, you can send clients an email at the end of certain months to remind them that their VAT return is due at the start of the following month. Therefore, they should send through their paperwork ASAP!

- **Diary management**: On my website I've got a section where clients can book time with me. You can use apps like Calendarly for this, but it's also built into Microsoft Office 365 nowadays, too. I set up this booking system while setting the boundaries I talked about earlier, because many client calls I receive are simply to book meetings with me. Similarly, I ensure clients know that I make use of my voicemail, and regularly check it. This means they feel safe being able to leave a message, knowing that I'll almost certainly receive it today, or at the latest tomorrow. Personally, I check my voicemail three times a day, on a similar schedule to checking my emails.

- **Social media scheduling**: You can build your client base online nowadays, and a good social media presence is ideal for this. You need to post regularly, so that the algorithm picks up what you're saying and shares it widely. To do this, I spend around an hour at the beginning of the week writing daily social media posts, and then schedule them to be posted across that week. I use Facebook and LinkedIn's own tools to schedule my posts but tools like Hootsuite are also available. Remember to schedule time to reply to any comments on your posts.

Time out

I mentioned at the start of this chapter how you're a team of one, but you have many different roles. You do need to factor in time to manage your business, outside of your work tasks.

For example, you might spend a day a month on marketing (although it's also worth remembering that, for some tasks like web development, it can simply be a more effective application of your time to get third-party support).

So, ensure you take time out for these tasks, and that it's built into your schedule. Often these tasks are around business growth, so they're equally important compared to the bread-and-butter tasks such as the bookkeeping, or communicating with clients.

More than this, however, remember to take time out occasionally to both reward yourself, and to take stock. You're the manager of yourself, and a role of the manager is to pat their employees on the back and say: Good work!

This can be for things you might consider trivial. For example, if you've just finished a really long bank reconciliation, release your inner manager and say: I did a good job. Now it's time to reward myself with a nice coffee and perhaps a quick break in the garden with the book you're reading.

Managers also sometimes give their teams treats as rewards when milestone goals are achieved. I once worked at a place where, as 4pm drew close on the day that marked the end of each month, the manager would hand out beers to everybody in the office. I'm not recommending boozing in the office, but something like a cake, or other treat, is not a bad idea once you've signed-off periodic monthly, quarterly or yearly tasks, like completing the VAT returns, or sending off the final Self Assessment tax return.

Have time out with your family, or children, or friends. Don't lose sight of the fact that we've chosen a bookkeeping lifestyle because we wanted time for this. We shouldn't live to work. We work to live! It's all about getting that balance right.

Above all, in your time out periods, ensure that your inner manager reminds you of the "why" we talked about in the previous chapter. Remember why you're doing this, and the value that it provides for you. Give yourself a pep talk! Look out of the window and remind yourself how the view is so much better than a stuffy corporate office where you don't have any freedom!

Think about how far you've come in your own business, and how well it's going.

WORKDAY
WEDNESDAY

In this chapter we look at the nitty-gritty of an actual working day. Later in the chapter, I'm going to share an idealised version of my own personal calendar, so you can see what it looks like.

Before we begin, though, let's take an overview of what a bookkeeper hopes to achieve each day.

Those new to bookkeeping might assume we're driven by immediate client needs in that the client tells us to do something, and we do it—including periodic tasks like reconciliation, or payroll, or VAT accounting, that we don't need prompting to do.

This isn't quite accurate.

What we're driven by are *results for our clients*. We're driven by completing things for them, such as ensuring the VAT Return is complete, accurate and submitted on time.

How you manage the individual tasks that contribute to this result is up to you. And it's important to get this right in order to avoid stress, and work at your best potential.

All clients are different, and have different needs. You will have uncovered these in your onboarding process. And some clients may demand more of your time than others.

But ultimately, the tasks are all similar, and knowing this can help you organise your day.

Bunching

A key component of my working day is what I call bunching, although you might also hear it called batching.

The principle is simple: group the same kind of tasks together, and ensure you have a slot in your day when this can be done, plus time later to process the output, if required.

More than this, however, is the fact bunching helps you get into a single mindset in which it's easier to complete things quickly and efficiently. Bunching means you're less likely to forget any small details required within the process, either. Essentially, you're turning all those small tasks into one large task.

Compare this to an ad-hoc way of working where you randomly pick-up small tasks. It's tiring because your mind is constantly leaping from one thing to another. And it's prone to creating errors, too.

Here's an example of my bunching. I schedule time where, morning and afternoon, I upload receipts from clients that I've received during the day, via emails or saved into Dropbox, straight to AutoEntry.

So, the process might be that they get uploaded to AutoEntry at the start of the day, with an hour set aside later for processing everything and pushing it through to the right client accounting software. This then means I know what I need to know to respond to client emails I read at lunchtime (and, if you recall from my earlier discussion of time management, I check my emails only three times a day—and outside of this time Microsoft Outlook is closed).

I also mentioned in the previous chapter something similar to the above, which is that the first week in the month is when I upload all my client bank statements to AutoEntry. This then gives me time so that I am them ready for checking the VAT Returns are correct, and they've got all their matching invoices, for example.

Similarly, if you have payroll tasks then lump them together, to ensure you do them at the same time.

Data processing

A profound realisation about bookkeeping is that, ultimately, we're a kind of highly knowledgeable and specialist data processor.

We receive and collect the data, we process it, and we then often must try and find the missing data! We then have to finalise the data according to whatever schedule is required for our clients' compliance, such as monthly, quarterly or yearly.

... we have to be data magicians when it comes to sourcing the data ...

Throughout everything, we have to ensure the data is high quality and, of course, accurate.

Again, this highlights why bunching is such a powerful technique. We'll be using the same tools to manage this data for all clients, such as AutoEntry. And we can be in the right mindset as we process data.

It can also mean we have to be data magicians when it comes to sourcing the data. Although the processes remain the same, and are repeated month on month, this component can add complexity.

For example, the number of e-commerce businesses exploded during the Covid pandemic, and I saw an increase in the number of e-commerce clients I have.

I might be gathering data from Shopify websites, or from payment and fulfilment services like Stripe, Klarna, Zettle and PayPal. Open Banking is obviously an awesome thing in terms of getting hold of banking data.

Prior to this Brexit changed how we accessed things like VAT data, too.

We have to be proficient in all of this, just as we are with our core accounting software. We need to understand how to output reports and connect them up to the accounting software. Sometimes this isn't possible, so we need to know how to deal with that, too.

For example, some of the above services provide settlement figures but these don't represent 100% of the sales figures, so you need to delve into the figures and find out fees, and then balance it all off.

And don't mention foreign transactions, which add exchange rates and additional fees to deal with!

That's why I used the term data magician earlier! Often, we have to think out of the box to find the most efficient ways to get the data into the accounting software.

Sometimes clients connect things up wrong for you too (PayPal is notorious for this), and you'll need to sort that out.

Open Banking is exploding at the moment and allowing all kinds of tricks with financial and accounting data. We're used to it being about bank account data flowing into the accounting software, but Open Banking is actually more powerful and can be about monitoring data moving out of the account, too.

There's lots of new apps built around this, and we need to keep our eyes on it. For example, some apps can even match email correspondence to banking transactions, which could be transformational in terms of our core tasks.

Clients are also discovering new apps powered by Open Banking, such as Crezco and Apron. We need to keep on top of this, too!

As a kind of data processor, we also have to be aware of rules and regulations around data protection, also!

Monotasking

Bookkeeping involves juggling lots of tasks for multiple clients. Because of this, everybody thinks we're multitaskers. But I find it's better to concentrate on single tasks and get them finished before moving onto the next.

Why? Well, if you try to complete two or three tasks at a time, there's a chance you won't be able to complete one or more of them. Or perhaps you simply won't give it the full attention it needs. Because your client is expecting that task to be completed, you'll find that the incomplete task escalates, and escalates, and escalates. In short, you're making problems for yourself.

Some people like to create lists of tasks that must be completed, and work their way through them. This could involve 20 or 30 tasks, with the knowledge that the individual will only complete a couple in a given day.

I'd advise against this. Instead, I'd advise setting a realistic goal of having two or three tasks that you know you'll complete that day.

Outside of blocking, as described earlier, my own system is to use sticky notes onto which I write tasks. This works for me. Each night before I shut down my computer, I write the tasks for the next day on these three sticky notes.

I use three different colours: pink, green and yellow. Pink is most urgent, followed by green. The task on the yellow note is the one I do when I'm sure that pink and green have been completed!

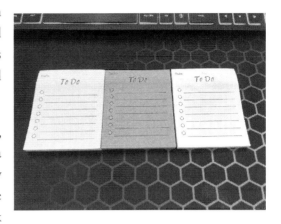

Ultimately, this is a form of time planning, and it can be difficult to perfect such a system. I made mistakes setting up my system, and you will, too. But the more you do it, the better you will get at it. Stick with it, because it's a core skill to have.

Managing software

Once again, much of your success here is going to be down to how you manage the software you use. I'm a great believer that if you pay for something, then you should learn it inside out and use it to its fullest ability.

I've never known any software not to evolve as time goes on. The version of Microsoft Office we have today is radically different to what we had a decade ago, for example. It's had thousands of new features added, some of which have changed entirely how we use the apps. I mentioned in the previous chapter how Microsoft Outlook's automation features can be useful, as just one example.

Most software lives in the cloud nowadays, in fact, and this means the rate at which new features are added has really started to speed up. With some apps you can expect to see new features released on a monthly basis.

You need to keep on top of this. It's not difficult. You'll find updates listed in the help pages for the app, for example. Sometimes you have to search for release notes. Sometimes you'll be told immediately when you access the updated app, via a pop-up window. There's often training materials available, like YouTube videos (even if these are produced by enthusiastic third parties who are simply fans of the app).

Standard operating procedures

Here are two other tips that you might like to consider when managing your working day that I refer to as my standard operation procedures, or SOPs:

- **Continuity of practice agreement**: It's good practice to setup an agreement with a fellow accountant or bookkeeper, who can take over your client books if anything happens to you. In my case, the fellow accountant has access should she need it in an emergency. Obviously, this is communicated to all my new clients when I onboard them, and is baked into my contracts, too.

- **Client filing:** You should aim to keep everything together for each client. This can be literally in a file within a filing cabinet, but I use practice management software. I record everything to help me remember details, no matter how small. Does the client prefer me to use a particular pronunciation of their name? I put it in there! If a client contacts me then I make a note against their file. I also include in there any peculiarities about a client's accounting, such as if they have unusual VAT arrangements because of overseas purchases, or sales that affect deliveries.

Daily schedule

As I mentioned earlier, my days are split into chunks. This includes chunks dedicated just to me not doing anything work-related, such as 60 or 90 minutes for me to grab some lunch. Similarly, I like to attend webinars. These are always good to boost Continuing Professional Development (CPD) points, but in recent times there's been lots to learn about topics like Anti-Money Laundering (AML), too. I've noticed that these tend to be delivered around lunchtime (presumably to encourage people to attend easily!). Therefore, I can build even ad-hoc events like this into my daily schedule because they're relatively predictable.

Here's an example of my weekly calendar.

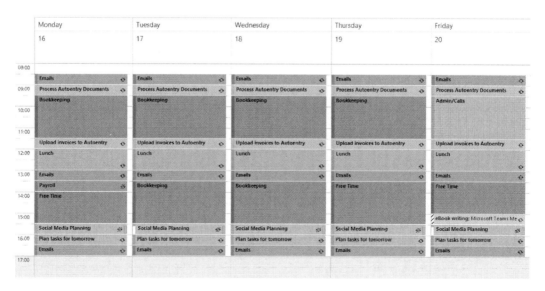

THROWBACK THURSDAY

In this chapter, we look at the processes around reviewing what you're doing at both an immediate, personal level, and also at a higher level.

We do this not only to make any necessary improvements, but also to protect ourselves from going off the path we carefully carved out in the first chapter, when we defined our "why".

There's a skill to reviewing yourself because it's like attempting to change the wheels on a car as it's driving along at 30MPH!

A fluid industry

Outsiders might suggest that bookkeeping and accounting in general are unchanging.

Surely, what a bookkeeper does today is pretty much the same as what they might've done 100 years ago? It's just about getting the numbers right… Right?

Yes, and no. You're managing the ledger, helping ensure compliance, and you might be taking care of other tasks, such as payroll. But ours is an industry where we make personal connections, and this means how we approach the work, and how we carry it out, is unique.

Furthermore, the world of tax legislation and accounting requirements can be surprisingly fluid. Every few years there are new Making Tax Digital requirements, for example, that affect the core taxation systems used by millions. Sometimes these inspire other changes, such as the 2023/2024 basis period reforms.

And, of course, technology is always improving. Unless you've only been skim reading thus far, you'll already know how I believe we have to be intimately connected with the technology that empowers us.

Keeping on top of all these things is a vital skill.

I hate to bring it up again, but the Covid lockdown and pandemic perfectly illustrated all three of these issues. Here in the UK, many people had to learn overnight about furloughing. They had to learn how to complete the forms so funding could get to the right people. There were new tax rates for the catering and hospitality industries, too.

Meanwhile, a home working revolution took place, and we all embraced technology to allow this to happen. I discussed this in previous chapters, but there was a real gear change at that time in how bookkeepers operated—and the potential for the future, too.

As bookkeepers, we need to keep one step ahead of all of this. You need to be evaluating the world and considering ways that we may need to respond. To do this, we review what we do constantly. We keep evolving.

It's up to us to learn those changes so that we can then adapt them into the way that we're working so we reap the benefits—whether it's for us to ensure we stay true to our "why", whether it's for time management, or whether it's for our client service levels.

Responsive bookkeeping

The question becomes: How do we not just keep up but also ensure we're ahead of it all?

Well, our industry provides a way: Continuous Professional Development, or CPD.

You should speak to your awarding body about their recommendations and requirements. With the Institute of Certified Bookkeepers (ICB), as one example, there's a requirement for members to get 30 CPD points per year. These are split into two categories: structured, and unstructured. Structured CPD points include things like attending training courses or attending branch meetings. Unstructured points include reading educational or technical materials, or even just taking on a new client.

But even with a keen eye on boosting your CPD count, it's not always easy to keep on top of changes and developments, especially when you're on your own. After all, it's not like you might have colleagues who pick-up on these things and share them amongst the team.

Other sources of learning could include HMRC updates, like the Agent Update emails, and the various webinars that HMRC runs. It could mean watching the various webinars that software vendors provide, or reading their blogs and PDF guides. The Sage Advice blog from Sage is particularly good. There are also some terrific and independent industry resources like XU Magazine that are free.

Be aware that some of these can officially count towards your CPD, too. For example, reading an article in XU magazine counts towards your CPD. You may find the same is true of the free webinars some software vendors provide.

You can also take advantage of social media. I'll discuss this more in the next chapter, because I find it an incredibly powerful tool. But a quirky post discussing around topic will often invite feedback from others, and open doors to sources of new information. You just have to find the right tribe—and again, I'll discuss this soon!

Throughout it all, we shouldn't forget that as a profession, bookkeepers are more resilient than we realise. Plus, it's vital to keep a positive frame of mind. Take, for example, the huge artificial intelligence breakthroughs that are now finding their way into the apps we use. A lot of people are scared of this, but for me, I know that's it's going to help us in a positive way.

We start fearing things when we stop reviewing and keeping on top of things. When we stop doing what we're doing and start panicking, we can forget why we actually became a bookkeeper.

How to self-review

When it comes to the finer details of reviewing yourself and what you do, it can initially be pretty difficult. I don't mind telling you that it's still something I'm working on, even though my practice is mature. But I believe constructive self-examination is a muscle that you can develop so that it becomes stronger. There might even be a day when it comes second nature.

My first piece of advice is general and basic: Don't review yourself against another person, or another business! Even though they might seem similar, the nature of bookkeeping could mean they're completely different compared to what you do and how you do it.

... don't review yourself against another person, or another business! ...

Plus, their reasons for being a bookkeeper might be entirely different to yours!

There are also a small number in our industry who like to boast about being very high earners. Again, be careful how you respond to this!

Instead, review against yourself and your journey so far. Look at what you've done previously, and look at what improvements you've already made, plus those that you can make. Going back to the opening chapter, you decided the "why" of your entry into bookkeeping. This is all you need to keep in mind.

How are you coping? How can you change things to make life better?

In the previous chapter I discussed standard operation procedures, or SOPs. If nothing else these act as a kind of backup for client service and interactions, and you should have one for every client.

It's with self-reviewing that they again show how incredibly useful they can be.

To remind you, your SOPs mean you should aim to keep everything together for each individual client. I record everything to help me remember details, no matter how small. If a client contacts me then I make a note against their file. I also include in there any peculiarities about a client's accounting, such as if they have unusual VAT arrangements because of overseas purchases, or sales that affect deliveries

The SOPs provide a way to review yourself and our client, if nothing else. You should look at them periodically outside of direct client interactions.

Are you undertaking tasks or procedures manually for that client that can now be done via software? Don't forget to take in consideration HMRC and changing government rules and how they will affect the client in future. For example, they've recently changed many dates for when you have to do Self Assessment.

Consider in your review how you communicate with the client, too.

In short, how is dealing with that particular client impacting you? Does anything need to change as a matter of urgency before you get into some kind of difficulty? Or, quite simply, can things be done better?

Remember: You're doing this for your own benefit, so that your work aligns with your "why". Taking constructive feedback from clients is certainly very important, but generating and taking it from yourself so that you're able to enjoy your work is even more vital.

Listening to your gut

Constructive feedback can come from a number of sources. One that shouldn't be ignored is simply your own gut feelings.

Recently I had somebody phone me up and enquire about my services. As always, I had a good chat with them. In these calls I try get a measure of them and gauge how well I might be able to work with them.

They soon started dictating to me when and how we should work together, and do business. I immediately had a bad feeling and was brave enough to say, sorry, I'm unable to assist them. I was able to recommend somebody else who I thought would be more suitable.

I had one client in particular, some time ago, where my gut feeling had been just to walk away after I began working for them. But I ignored it. I thought, well, I can fix this. I can keep the relationship going. But in the end, it just became a nightmare. It was pushing me towards throwing in the towel and walking away from this amazing business I'd created.

I discussed the matter online in some of my social media groups, where I chat to other accounting professionals. They were full of constructive feedback.

My gut feeling had been right. My peers online had corroborated it.

I not only got rid of that client, but also learned a difficult yet invaluable lesson about the importance of listening to myself and building gut feelings into my self-review processes—as well as sharing with others.

There are accounting professionals who claim there's no bad client, and that it's just a matter of training them to be better. I have to disagree. Maybe in large practices it can be argued that training clients might work, but if it's just you, as a sole practitioner, then you have to protect yourself. After all, nobody else will!

At the end of the day, it comes down to this: Don't let somebody else control your business for you. Don't let them control you, either.

Once you know what kind of people you like to work with, then my advice is not to deviate from that—and don't ignore your gut feeling, because it can save a lot of stress and pain down the line, for both you and the client.

If you get the right clients, in that you feel in your gut that they're right, then quite the opposite happens. With my clients I have all sorts of quirky conversations, and when I meet their deadlines in a clear and efficient manner, the feeling of satisfaction I get is worth its weight in gold. It makes it all worth it!

Embracing the challenge

None of this is to say that client work can't be difficult or challenging, of course!

Part of my own self review process is to continually seek out challenges. I'm constantly looking for new rock faces that I can climb to the top of, and this is important because we need to keep things fresh and maintain our interest in what we're doing.

I love the fact that I've got a large client whose accounts are really, really quite intense. Every month they're a challenge to complete because I need to gather many different sources of information. At the end it's incredibly rewarding to think that I've got together 2-3,000 transactions and done a good, old-fashioned bank reconciliation at the end. Processing them all is almost therapeutic.

I've already mentioned how we have to review technology, and, for me, this is another element that keeps things fresh and interesting. I love technology. If I can find some new technology that's going to make it a little bit more exciting to do the bookkeeping, it really enthuses me!

FEELGOOD
FRIDAY

Congratulations! You've made it to the end of the virtual week that comprises this book.

You might recall how, way back on Motivational Monday, I talked about how you're managing a team of one. Well, now's the time to put on your manager's hat and evaluate your team's performance, as well as align your team for the coming week so that you start next Monday on the best foot.

Also in this chapter we'll look at the benefits of support networks, and how social media in particular can be a powerful tool for sole practitioners when it comes to good mental health—and ensuring you feelgood all week round.

Reviewing and rewarding

Every Friday I look at my calendar and look at what's happening next week. It's a little like a team planning session, but the team is just me!

It's also the time at which I take the opportunity to look at the week's events that have just passed—whether that's on the calendar or my To Do list—and pat myself on the back for having achieved what I've done.

This is just so important, and you should reward yourself however you feel is warranted. A chocolate bar, perhaps, or spending a little time reading. I'm a fan of the sport of MotoGP. It just so happens that practice rounds are broadcast on TV on a Friday morning, so I reward myself with an hour or two of watching TV!

Of course, there will be things you haven't been able to tick-off the list, for whatever reason. Now's the time to try and work out why and reschedule as required. Is there something you can change or adjust to make the task easier?

It might just be biting the bullet and forcing the task through, and it's on Friday that you should remember all the times you did this.

For example, recently I had a big task that I've been putting off for some time. Eventually, I just turned on my computer one morning and got on with it immediately. I didn't even think about it beforehand.

Now, just as I was finishing this terrible task, I got a notification that I'd won a prize in a LinkedIn promotion: A Fortnum and Mason hamper!

Was this some kind of karma rewarding me? Maybe! But it made me connect the dots in my own working life and realise that getting those difficult tasks out of the way is a kind of reward in itself.

For starters, the rest of the day was a piece of cake by comparison. But also, I was rewarded when it came to my mental health. This task had been getting me down. Once it had gone, I felt so much better.

And so, on Fridays, I make sure to include taking stock of tasks like this. I get a second wave of good feeling from realising that I'd climbed those mountains—and got to the top. It's so important to be as detailed as this when you think back over the week.

You should add into this everything else that's happening in your life. Perhaps that's managing the kids and your spouse, taking care of the home, and all while managing your own business and working all day.

You did well to get to Friday. You've achieved a lot. You've worked hard. Nobody else but you knows this, so therefore it's down to you to feel good about yourself.

Say it loud and say it proud: Well done, me!

Planning

It's at the end of the week that you can align yourself for the next week, too, so that you're not stretching yourself in the wrong way. This involves the same techniques we've discussed in the Workload Wednesday chapter.

But now we have actual notes and feedback from the past week to inform that same bunching of tasks, in which we group similar tasks together for efficiency.

This is where I come back to the sticky notes system I mentioned in the Workload Wednesday chapter, and how I grade tasks based on their urgency.

For example, you might have a client phone on Friday about something that, to the client, is very urgent. They want a call with you on Monday, but perhaps that's the day you dedicate to processing paperwork for bookkeeping.

Breaking your flow and your schedule for a non-routine task like a client call can be devastating. It's bad for your mental health if you have to switch modes, but it also jeopardises your time management. Calls can be a huge thief of time.

To set your priorities in the coming week, consider what are the urgent things—the things you cannot change that have to happen next week. Examples include tasks attached to deadlines, but there could be vital calls with people to advance projects.

After all, this isn't about avoiding things outside of your normal task bunching. It's just understanding the importance of upcoming requirements, and avoiding overbooking yourself. Remember what I said a few chapters ago: You can't pour from an empty cup. You have limited resources, and you need to spend them wisely, and with forethought.

Learning to say no is a vital skill for a sole practitioner. You may have realised by now that the theme running throughout this book is remaining in control of what you do. You should never, ever relinquish this.

Support networks

As this book comes to a close, I want to share one of the most important things that enabled me to both start and carry on with my work as a bookkeeper.

It remains true to this very day.

It's finding your tribe. It's putting in place a network that does everything from help you when you've a technical query, to sharing your highs when you have success, plus everything in-between.

Peer-to-peer support is something that's never taught in a textbook. For many of us, it's something where we've tried and tested things, and often failed.

I tried real-life networking events, dashing around the country. They didn't work for me and, anyway, the travelling meant I never had time to do any work! Covid put a stop to many of these events at the time my business was growing, in any event.

... every day is a school day for us as bookkeepers, and every day we learn something new ...

Online communities offer something different. It was where I found lots of people in one place, all with different abilities and experience—but all in the same boat as me. It provides a way of sharing first-hand experience that I've simply not found anywhere else.

Every day is a school day for us as bookkeepers, and every day we learn something new. Online communities help with this, too.

But there was an issue when I first started looking online for my tribe. I joined a few communities but the answers I got back to questions were just horrible. Often these places were inhabited with old-fashioned accountants and bookkeepers, who had gained notoriety because they were experts—but they were also quite negative, and often rude.

So, with a few friends I'd already made online in previous Facebook groups, we decided we'd create our own community: Accountant & Bookkeepers Support UK. It currently has over 12,000 members—and you're invited to join, too!

That community has grown purely based on the fact no question is ever considered silly. All questions are comments are warranted and are valid. People can also post anonymously, which can help those who want to keep things confidential. I'm a huge fan of this because it enables people to ask for help when they might not otherwise.

As an example, somebody recently posted about issues with a client and the response from the community was almost unanimous: Walk away. This was a vital perspective that the sole practitioner posting the message just couldn't see. This person was also down and stressed, and our response helped with her mood, too.

I'm a great believer in the saying that you must always help somebody, because you might be the only person that does. In our community, people like me can reach out and say, "You're not alone". We can provide that little bit of sunshine. We can tell them that, even if we can't help them, we can still listen to them.

We're all sole practitioners and communities like this are one of the biggest mental health boosts. We all face the same challenges, daily. We might be sole practitioners, but we can operate as a team.

In other words, this is another way of using software as an employee. You're using the online community for virtual support, just like you would colleagues or other team members in a work environment. You can resonate with them. You can have really open discussions about what does and doesn't work. You benefit from that huge range of knowledge and skills.

WEEKEND
REFLECTIONS

Although sole practitioners work on their own, we're part of many larger communities. These may be our awarding bodies, or they may be ad-hoc groups that we set-up amongst ourselves.

If you haven't already, I'd like to invite you to join two communities I run:

- **The Maverick Revolution**: At The Maverick Revolution, your voice will forever be heard, and you'll find a nurturing community to foster your business and your style. Together, we'll conquer obstacles and shatter our ambitions. This is a community designed to support the Lone Rangers of the accounting world – the superheroes that are Sole Practitioners. To learn more, visit https://www.bewitchingbks.co.uk/#maverick.

- **The Accountant & Bookkeepers Support**: This is the Facebook group I referenced in the previous chapter, and it offers support to UK bookkeepers and accountants, whether they've been in practice for a while, only have just started (or even thinking of starting!). Our aim is to offer support, help, tips and advice without any kind of judgement. To join, visit https://www.facebook.com/groups/accountantandbookkeeperssupport.

But now, as my book comes to an end, there's only one thing left to say: Good luck. If you follow what I've described, you'll be entering what I believe to be one of the very best professions. It's a way to make a great living while working in the way you want. I wouldn't change it for the world!

AUTOENTRY: LEAVE THE DATA ENTRY TO AUTOMATION

My thanks go to AutoEntry for sponsoring this guide. I've been incredibly happy to work with AutoEntry because, as I've explained in the pages of this book, it's perhaps the most important software tool that I use daily as an accounting professional.

It allows me to automatically extract data from my clients' statements, invoices and receipts. There are many more features on top of this, of course, not least of which is the unique supplier statement reconciliation. This alone saves me hours if not days each month, on top of the incredible amount of time AutoEntry already saves.

Accuracy is increased compared to manually entering the data by hand, too.

I also like how there's no contract required with AutoEntry, and I just pay for what I need on a month-by-month basis. I can cancel at any time. All the features I require are included as standard, such as unlimited client companies and storage, and are not optional extras.

If you've never used AutoEntry before, you can get a free trial by entering the link below into your web browser. You get 25 free credits—enough to scan the data from 25 invoices or receipts—plus 50% off your subscription for the first six months.

Full disclosure: This is via AutoEntry's Partner Programme, in which I earn free credits for referring people. But I'm sure you'll agree that it's an incredibly good offer!

data.autoentry.com/signup/partner/87FAF

How AutoEntry works

1 **Capture**

Simply email, scan or snap your invoices, receipts and statements with the AutoEntry mobile or desktop app.

2 **Categorise**

Categorise your financial documents once and never have to do it again. AutoEntry remembers the categories based on your data.

3 **Publish**

We've got this! AutoEntry does the rest and publishes financial data through to accounts software.

www.autoentry.com

ABOUT THE AUTHOR

Natasha Everard is a passionate bookkeeper with a deep love for helping others. Her journey in the field began with a Modern Apprenticeship back in 1997. Since then, she's been on a mission to learn and evolve.

She believes in supporting others and these principles guide every aspect of her work. She's a firm advocate for striving to make a positive impact in her community, and beyond.

When Natasha is not bookkeeping or supporting others you can find her watching Motobike racing. She lives and breathes MotoGP, World Superbikes and British Superbikes!

www.bewitchingbks.co.uk

Printed in Great Britain
by Amazon

33187371R00035